Entrepreneur's GUIDE

TO BUILDING A SOLID LEGAL FOUNDATION

Dayna Thomas, Esq.

This publication is not to be taken as legal advice and is for educational purposes only. Please consult with an attorney for legal advice on your particular situation.

"Dayna helped me to establish my company, and she made the process incredibly easy! Thankful to have her in my corner on this journey of entrepreneurship."

- **Nicole Myers**, Owner – Myers & Associates, LLC

"Dayna Thomas is a purpose-driven superstar who values people and their dreams. She is a phenomenal person of impact, and she knows her stuff."

- **Victor Cobb**, Screenplay Writer

"Dayna Thomas, Esq. is communicative, knowledgeable, sharp, and superb. She is a very smart and compassionate woman who knows her field. In a short period of time, Attorney Thomas gained my trust because above all, she is a great human being who genuinely cares for and represents the best interests of her clients. I am proud to be represented by such a powerful woman in her field."

- **Ann-Marie Hammond**, Finance Professional

"I have worked with Dayna Thomas, Esq. for some time now and she is by far an impeccable attorney and business consultant. The timeliness of her responses, accuracy of her counsel, and her sincere belief in me as a client continues to strengthen our attorney-client relationship, resulting in a dynamic team."

- **Terrence Hight, Jr.**, Founder and CEO – Connected Care, LLC

"Dayna is one of the most thorough and efficient attorney's I've ever worked with. She handled my contract negotiations with the utmost professionalism, communicated to me clearly and effectively, and broke down realistic probabilities and outcomes. She went above and beyond, taking the time to truly understand my needs and provided everything requested and more."

- **Matthew Braham**, CEO – Noel Braham Entertainment

"Dayna has gained my full trust and loyalty. She has helped me significantly on more than one occasion and I can honestly say that I do not associate myself with any other business lawyer but her. She is very intelligent and knowledgeable about her field of work."

- **Jade Moore**, Founder and CEO – Angela Moore Productions, LLC

Entrepreneur's GUIDE

TO BUILDING A SOLID LEGAL FOUNDATION

Copyright © 2016 by The Law Office of Dayna Thomas, LLC

All rights reserved. No part of this publication may be reproduced, distributed or transmitted in any form or by any means, including photocopying, recording, or other electronic or mechanical methods, without the prior written permission of the author, except in the case of brief quotations embodied in critical reviews and certain other noncommercial uses permitted by copyright law.

While the publisher and author have used their best efforts in preparing this book, they make no representations or warranties regarding the accuracy or completeness of the contents of this book. The publisher and author specifically disclaim any implied warranties of merchantability or fitness for a particular purpose, and make no guarantees whatsoever that you will achieve any particular result. Any examples that are presented herein do not necessarily represent what you should expect to achieve, as business success depends on a variety of factors. The advice and strategies contained in this book may not be suitable for your situation, and you should consult your own advisors as appropriate. The publisher and author shall not be held liable for any loss of profit or any other commercial damages, including but not limited to special, incidental, consequential, or other damages. We believe that transparency is important and we hold ourselves (and you) to a high standard of integrity. Thanks for reading.

Contact the author:
www.DaynaThomasLaw.com

All social media: @daynathomaslaw

ISBN: 978-0-692-80444-5

First Edition

Dedication

This book is dedicated to those individuals who know that their existence has more purpose than working for someone else their whole life; those individuals who have a burning desire to start their own business but fear is holding them back; those individuals who can't sleep because of all of the business ideas that flood their mind; those individuals that want to live a more fulfilled life by serving others with their unique skills and talents. I know what that feels like.

You have the power to make it happen.

Thank you for all of your support: Mom, Dad, my sisters - Kimera and Mariah, Antonisha Baker, Chris Ivory, my mentors, family, and friends.

TABLE OF CONTENTS

	Introduction	1
1.	Non-Disclosure Agreements	4
2.	Business Entity Structures	9
3.	Operating Agreements	15
4.	Contracts	22
5.	Employment	28
6.	Trademarks and Service Marks	36
7.	Copyright	44
8.	Patents	49
9.	Licensing	54
10.	Protecting Your Limited Liability	59
	Final Thought	63

Introduction

Deciding to start a business can be one of the best decisions in your life. Successful entrepreneurship comes with greater control over your time and ability to generate income, as well as an overall better quality of life. However, achieving such success certainly does not come easy and there are many factors to consider, obstacles to overcome, and mistakes to be made in order to realize that vision of abundance that you have for your life.

Unfortunately, many business owners only consider working with a lawyer when their business is in trouble; however, they fail to realize that if they covered their legal bases from the beginning, then their entrepreneurial journey would be a much smoother and more profitable ride.

I wrote this book because I know that entrepreneurs (and people in general) are often intimidated by the legal process and the legal aspects of business. When people hear the word "lawyer," they often think two things: (1) expense and (2) confusion. While it is true that quality legal services to build and protect your business are not cheap, its purpose is to save you money (and make you money) in the long-term, making it an investment rather than an expense.

Despite the fact that obtaining the services of an entrepreneurship attorney is critical to the business building process, I know that many new entrepreneurs are not in a position to allocate the required budget towards legal fees. That's why I have made it one of my goals to be more creative in getting basic legal information to aspiring and new entrepreneurs so that I can support them in their journey.

The legal aspects of business certainly cannot be taken lightly in your journey to and through entrepreneurship. Building a solid legal foundation for your business can be the difference between a booming business and a business bust. This book covers important legal topics that you must consider in order to give your business the best chance at long-term prosperity. My goal is to help give you the information you need to be confident as a current or future entrepreneur. If you're still on the fence about whether you should pursue entrepreneurship, remember this: The best way to predict the future, is to create it.

Entrepreneur's GUIDE

- 1 -

NON-DISCLOSURE AGREEMENTS

NON-DISCLOSURE AGREEMENTS

Protecting your business idea can be quite a task. Many people think that mere ideas are protectable by either copyright, trademark, or patents. However, that is not the case. It's important to have a way to keep your idea safe while you take steps to make it come to life. A non-disclosure agreement is a great way to achieve that. A non-disclosure agreement, also known as an NDA or a confidentiality agreement, is a legally-binding contract in which one or more parties agree not to disclose to others any confidential information that they have shared with each other. More than likely, you will have to share your business idea with others for it to grow from the idea phase to revenue-generating. Having each person or business you share it with sign a non-disclosure agreement can give you peace of mind during that process.

A non-disclosure agreement must be clear about what information is confidential and be all-inclusive, yet reasonable. For example, confidential information may include:

- The terms of proposals and agreements with the other party
- The terms of proposals and agreements with third parties

- Technical and business information
- Trade secrets
- Drawings and/or illustrations
- Patent searches
- Existing and/or contemplated products and services
- Research and development
- Designs, blueprints, and specifications
- Formulas
- Computer software
- Collections of data
- Business strategies and ideas
- Costs, profit, and margin information
- Finances and financial projections
- Customers and client lists
- Supplier lists
- Employee information
- Marketing strategies
- Sales data
- Inventory
- Expenditures
- Current and future business plans and models

What you include in your list of confidential information is often subject to the industry you are in, so be sure to consider other information that should be confidential for your business that others may not have to consider. For even greater protection, your non-disclosure agreement should state that the confidential information is not limited to the above list and that anything on the list is considered confidential information regardless if it is designated as such at the time of its disclosure.

It is equally important to include what is not considered confidential information because it is evidence that your non-disclosure agreement is reasonable and legally sound. Two important exclusions are (1) information which is, or later on becomes, known by the general public through no fault of the person you shared the information with, and (2) information discovered by the person you shared the information with prior to (or independent of) any involvement with you.

Your non-disclosure agreement should also require the other party to have their employees, affiliates, or others execute their own non-disclosure agreement if confidential information must be shared with them in order to achieve your business goals. You should obtain a copy of all third party non-disclosure agreements that relate to your confidential information.

Finally, your non-disclosure agreement should state how long the information should be kept confidential. This time period can be a number of years based on the timeline for business development, or can be until the confidential information is legitimately disclosed by you.

In the event that a person or entity that is bound by your non-disclosure agreement shares confidential information with a third party in violation of the agreement, you can get a court order to stop the violator from making any further disclosures (which is referred to as an "injunction"), as well as get monetary damages.

Entrepreneur's GUIDE

BUSINESS ENTITY STRUCTURES

BUSINESS STRUCTURES

Operating a business without a formal business structure exposes you to a great deal of personal liability. Having a formal business structure is crucial, largely because in general, the business owner(s) will not be personally liable for the debts of the company. This means that if the business cannot pay for its debts (such as business credit card debt or business loans), then the creditor cannot seek repayment from any of your personal assets such as your house, car, funds in your personal bank account, etc. The debt can only be repaid from the assets of the business, unless your limited liability has been compromised. (See Chapter 10 – Protecting Your Limited Liability).

There are several different types of business structures, the most common being sole proprietorships, limited liability companies, corporations, and partnerships. Each of these business structures offers different value to the owners, so choosing the right entity is an important primary step in launching your business. Here is a comparison of each common type:

Sole Proprietorship

- Personal Liability | Business owner has unlimited liability for business debts

- Formalities | Virtually none
- Management | Can only have one owner; very flexible management
- Taxation | Business is not taxed separately from the owner
- Recommended For | Businesses that only need the owner to operate; businesses that do not need funding or employees; business that do not deal with money

Limited Liability Companies (LLC)

- Personal Liability | Members are not typically liable for the debts of the LLC.
- Formalities | Formal meetings and minutes are not required; however, filing your annual state registration is required.
- Management | Management is flexible. Typically, an operating agreement outlines management duties.
- Taxation | By default, income and losses are passed-through to the members' individual tax returns. LLCs may also elect to be taxed as a C- or S-Corporation.
- Recommended For | Business owners wanting strong liability protection with minimal corporate formalities, the simplicity of pass-through taxation, and easy entity management.

| Business Entity Structures

C - Corporations

- Personal Liability | Shareholders are not typically liable for the debts of the corporation.

- Formalities | Formal board of directors, bylaws, shareholder meetings, and meeting minutes are required, as well as annual state registration.

- Management | Managed by the board of directors, who are typically elected by the shareholders. Directors appoint officers, who run the daily operations.

- Taxation | Taxed at the entity level. If dividends are distributed to shareholders, dividend income is also taxed at the individual level. This is called "double taxation."

- Recommended For | Businesses that want to issue stock or stock options to attract key employees or investment capital; businesses that are so profitable that they can share in tax advantages; businesses that don't mind adhering to the corporate formality requirements.

S - Corporations

- Personal Liability | Shareholders are not typically liable for the debts of the corporation.

- Formalities | Formal board of directors, bylaws, shareholder meetings, and meeting minutes are required, as well as annual state registration.

- Management | Managed by the board of directors, who are elected by the shareholders. Directors appoint officers, who run the daily operations.

- Taxation | No tax at the entity level. Income and losses are passed through to the shareholder.

- Limitations | Limited to 100 shareholders and can only have one class of stock. Stock can only be owned by individuals, estates, and certain types of trusts, and not by other companies.

- Recommended For | Owners wanting the liability protection of a corporation, with the simplicity of pass-through taxation, and don't mind adhering to the corporate formality requirements.

Partnerships

- Personal Liability | At least one owner has unlimited personal liability.

- Formalities | Relatively few formal requirements.

- Management | Flexible management and operational structure.

- Taxation | Income and losses are passed through to owners.

- Recommended For | Owners wanting minimal formalities, maximum flexibility, and not worried about personal liability.

Business Entity Structures

For most new entrepreneurs, a limited liability company is the best option. It protects against personal liability for business debts, and is flexible enough to allow you to manage your business in the way that you desire. There are very few corporate requirements which gives you the ability to focus on what's most important – growing your business!

Entrepreneur's GUIDE

- 3 -

OPERATING AGREEMENTS

OPERATING AGREEMENTS

A huge mistake that many business owners make, especially if they are in business with family or friends, is neglecting to execute an operating agreement. An operating agreement is an agreement between the members of the LLC regarding the affairs, conduct, management and operating procedure of the company. It provides a guideline for how the business will be run and how important decisions will be made. Many business partners make the mistake of failing to execute an operating agreement either because they (1) aren't willing to invest their money into having it properly drafted, (2) don't understand its importance, or (3) trust that they will always see eye-to-eye with each other. However, running your business without executing an operating agreement between yourself and your business partner(s) is a risk that no business owner should take. Without one, your state's default rules will apply, which may not reflect the intentions or desires of the LLC's members.

Ideally, each member of the LLC should have his or her own attorney to represent them during the negotiation of the operating agreement so that their individual interests are protected. Several important terms are included in a well-drafted operating agreement. A few of those terms are included below.

Capital Contributions

Among other things, the operating agreement states the current members of the LLC, as well as how much capital each member has contributed to the company, if any. A capital contribution is cash or assets given to a business entity in exchange for an equity interest or as part of an ongoing obligation. Unless otherwise specified in the operating agreement, a member's ownership interest is initially equal to his/her capital contribution. For instance, if an LLC has two members, and one contributed $60,000 to start the business and the other contributed $40,000, the first member would own 60 percent of the company, with the second member owning 40 percent.

The capital contributions section is also important because if, for example, your business needs funds for a new project, this part of the operating agreement will state how to require each member to contribute capital and what happens in the event that a member is financially unable to do so.

Members and Management

The operating agreement also states how to add new members to the LLC. Current members will likely want to have a say in who is able to share in ownership, so the operating agreement will detail how to make that decision. Likewise, the operating agreement provides for how members may withdraw or resign from the company.

Appointment of the LLC manager may also be included in the operating agreement. It will detail how managers are appointed as well as the manager's powers and authority. Some LLC's are member-managed, which means that all members of the LLC act as managers rather than one or some.

Regular and special voting structures are also included in the operating agreement. It lays out which types of decisions require a regular vote and which require a special vote. For example, deciding whether to change the principal place of business or enter into a business contract may require a regular vote (majority approval, for example). However, deciding to dissolve the company or change the nature of the business may require a special vote (such as unanimous approval).

In addition, the protocol for unforeseen circumstances such as death, incompetency, and/or bankruptcy of a member is also included in the operating agreement. By default, the state law where the LLC was formed determines the effect of a member's death, incompetency, and/or bankruptcy on the LLC. However, the members can alter this in the operating agreement if they desire.

Profits and Losses

A great benefit of having an operating agreement is that the members can designate how they want profits and losses to be shared. If it is not specified in the operating agreement, profits and losses are allocated in the same ratio as each member's ownership interest. This method of allocating profits and losses is the default method established by most state LLC laws. However, you can change this to any allocation ratio that you desire, regardless of capital contributions.

For example, if Member A's capital contribution is $60,000 and she does not help operate the business at all, and Member B's capital contribution is $40,000 and he manages the entire business, the operating agreement can override the state's default rule and both members can share in ownership 50-50 if they so desire, rather than 60-40 by default. In addition, the operating agreement will state when distributions of profits will be made and what type of vote is required, if any, to do so.

The operating agreement should also state how losses will be allocated. By default, losses are allocated to members in the same proportion as profits. However, the members can allocate losses in different proportions in the operating agreement if they choose to.

Transfer of Membership Interest

As mentioned above, current LLC members usually want to have a say in who can join the LLC as a member. This usually occurs by transfer of interest. Transfer of interest generally means the sale, conveyance, assignment, transfer, pledge, grant of a security interest in or otherwise disposition of all or part of a member's interest in the LLC. There may be different protocol for transfers to current LLC members and transfers to non-LLC members, depending on preference. The operating agreement states how a member's right to transfer will be granted and how to determine the value of the interest to be transferred.

A right of first refusal is a key term in the transfer of interest section of the operating agreement that is not granted by default. With transfers of membership interest, a right of first refusal is a contractual right that gives the members of the LLC the option to purchase all or some of the offered interest, according to specified terms, before the selling member is entitled to transfer the interest to someone outside of the LLC. This is a privilege for the current LLC members which allows them to increase their ownership interests rather than sharing interest with a new member.

As you can see, having a well-written operating agreement can provide great flexibility and control for LLC members. Rather than having to oblige to blanket state laws, the operating agreement is a way to ensure that your business will run how you want it to, and decisions will be made how you and your business partners desire.

# Entrepreneur's GUIDE

- 4 -

CONTRACTS

CONTRACTS

Having contracts for your business transactions is crucial; particularly contracts with your clients/customers and people or businesses that you collaborate with. It is so important that the terms of your agreements are put in writing; not only because it is a legal document that will be your evidence in court if there is a dispute, but also because it clearly sets the expectations of both parties.

Client Contracts

Clients are often the best source of referrals for your business. Therefore, it is important to make sure that you do all that you can to maintain a positive relationship with your clients. Along with providing excellent customer service, having a client agreement will help ensure that both parties are on the same page about what your product or service includes (and often more importantly, does not include), payment requirements, and other provisions that will help diffuse any misunderstanding.

Contracts with clients should state all of the "material" (legal jargon for important) terms of your agreement, which at minimum should include:

- The length of time of the relationship
- Description of the product or service provided
- Cost of the product or service
- Payment terms
- Delivery schedule
- Dispute resolution
- Termination
- Remedies for breach
- Refund policy
- Governing law

Contracts help to reduce miscommunication about what was expected or agreed to, and therefore, lead to a better working relationship. In the event of a dispute, going back to the contract is often a quick and easy way towards a resolution.

Outside of legal implications, having a client contract shows that you are professional, and inspires confidence in your clients because they will know that you take your business seriously. You will know upfront if there are any concerns about your business process, and can address them at the beginning of the relationship so that your client knows what to expect.

Overall, a proper contract with your clients can keep you out of expensive litigation, shield against unwarranted refunds, entitle you to payment for your product or service, and manage client expectations. The great thing is, with client contracts, you can have one template that you use for all (or most) of your clients, making it a great investment.

Collaborator Contracts

Collaborator contracts is my phrase for agreements with individuals or entities that you work or partner with in order to advance your business. Collaborators can include investors, community organizations, other companies, and advisors, to name a few.

Along with laying out the terms of your agreement to ensure mutual understanding, collaborator contracts are a great way to limit your business's exposure to liability for the other party's wrongful acts. Collaborators have to be careful that their working relationship is not considered a partnership in a court of law. If your business is considered a legal partner of another company, then your business may be liable for the wrongful acts of that company.

| Contracts

Generally, a partnership is a legal form of business operation between two or more individuals or entities who share management and profits. Naturally, when you work with a collaborator, you both may have a say in how the project is managed and share in the profits. However, a contract can protect against any ambiguities about whether the relationship is a partnership, and it can also be evidence in court that your business is not a partnership if legal disputes arise.

Indemnification

Indemnification provisions in collaborator contracts are also crucial. An indemnification provision is a clause in a contract under which one party (or both parties) commit to compensate the other (or each other) for any harm, liability, or loss arising out of the contract. For example, if Company A and Company B collaborate, and Company B breaches the contract, then the indemnification provision can require Company B to pay for the costs and expenses that Company A incurred as a result.

Collaborator contracts have key provisions that can ensure that you will not be financially liable for the wrongful acts of the other party, and can give you peace of mind when collaborating with others to grow your business and brand.

Privacy Policy and Terms and Conditions

Two other important business contracts are privacy policies and terms and conditions. If you collect people's information on your website, then you must have a privacy policy. There are various state and federal laws that have specific rules on privacy policy requirements. Even if your particular state does not require a privacy policy, if the state that your visitor browses from does, then you are likely subject to that state's privacy policy law. A privacy policy ensures your visitors that you will not sell or give out personal/private information to any other parties. Not only is it required, it will make your visitors feel safe and secure.

You should also have a terms and conditions agreement on your website. The terms and conditions acts as a contract between you and all of your site visitors. The terms can vary depending on the type of business you have, but the essence is that the terms protect your company from potential legal action by visitors to your website and puts visitors on notice that you (or your business) own all of the content on the site. This helps protect against copyright infringement and sets the rules on how your site is to be used.

Entrepreneur's GUIDE

- 5 -

EMPLOYMENT

Employment

New entrepreneurs generally do not have employees when they first start. The most common scenario is one person running the operation and building from the ground up. Overtime as the business grows, it will be important to meet the demands of a flourishing business. One way to do that is to hire employees.

Employment Agreements

The expectations that you have for your employees should be clear to avoid disputes or delays that could hinder the progression of your business. An employment agreement is a great tool to achieve that. An employment agreement is a contract that sets forth the terms of the relationship between an employer and an employee. Employment agreements are not required; however, in many cases, it provides greats benefit to the employer.

Along with describing the responsibilities of both the employer and the employee as a result of the hire, a good employment agreement should include:

- The duration of the job

| Employment

- Benefits (such as health insurance, vacation leave, and disability leave) that the employee will receive
- A non-compete provision
- Protection of your confidential information and client lists
- Grounds for termination
- Your ownership of the employee's work product
- Dispute resolution

Having an employment agreement with your employees can be very useful if you want more control over what the employee can and cannot do. For example, if finding a replacement for your employee will be very costly and time-consuming, an employment agreement can state a specific length for the employment period, or require the employee to give you advance written notice of his/her intent to leave. Although you cannot require an employee to stay and continue to work for you (prohibited by the 13th Amendment which abolished slavery and involuntary servitude), an employee is likely to comply with a written agreement in order to avoid a penalty.

In addition, if the employee will be exposed to confidential information or trade secrets within your business, an employment agreement can require the employee to keep all of that information confidential and prevent them from using it to their advantage or to the detriment of the business. For example, if your employees will have access to your customer lists, the employment agreement will prohibit them from using the customer lists in any manner, especially to drive customers away from your business and towards their own.

You can also use employment agreements to entice highly-skilled candidates to work for you instead of the competition. By laying out the terms of your agreement, candidates will feel a stronger sense of job security, which can motivate them to work for you.

Non-compete Provisions

Employment agreements also allow you to include restrictions on the employee competing with your business post-employment. Employees normally have access to information that they could potentially use to compete with your business. With an employment agreement, you can include a non-compete provision which can prevent the employee from either working for a competitor or starting a competing business.

The key to having an enforceable non-compete provision is making sure that it is reasonable in duration and scope. The reasonableness of duration will depend on the facts of each situation, but generally, a reasonable duration is how long the threat to your business lasts. Some states generally have a set time period (two years, for example). Scope includes what is being restricted, and the geographic location in which the restriction applies, which must also be reasonable.

For example, if your business has one location in a small town and the job requires low-skill level and minimal access to trade secrets, it may not be reasonable to prevent the employee from working for a competitor in a different state. However, if you have several business locations on the east coast and the job is for a high-level employee who makes strategic business decisions on a daily basis, then a non-compete provision will likely be enforceable for that region.

Although having an agreement with your employees has its benefits, it can also limit your flexibility as the employer because the contract binds both parties. Therefore, if you decide that you want to make adjustments to the terms of your agreement, it may require some negotiation with the employee so that you are not in breach of contract. It's important to consider both the pros and cons of having an employment agreement, and to have it drafted in a way that allows for minor (or even major) amendments. Depending on the terms, an employment contract may also limit your ability to terminate an employee, if your business operates in a state that recognizes "at-will" employment.

At-Will Employment

When determining the terms of your employment agreement, or even whether you should require one at all, consider whether your state is an at-will employment state. At-will employment means that employees without a contract can have their employment terminated by either party at any time and for *almost* any reason. Those reasons, however, must be in accordance with federal and state law. For example, an employer cannot terminate an employee based on race, gender, disability, age, sexual orientation, and other characteristics, which would be deemed as unlawful discrimination.

Even in at-will employment states, there are additional exceptions to the rule which could expose your business to liability as a result of terminating an employee, so be sure to consider your particular state's laws.

Independent Contractor Status

Business owners must beware to correctly identify whether the individuals providing services to their business are employees or independent contractors. Employment status affects many issues such as tax implications, employment benefits, and liability. Generally, for employees, you must withhold income taxes, withhold and pay Social Security and Medicare taxes, and pay federal and state unemployment tax on wages. However, for independent contractors, you generally do not have to withhold or pay those taxes. In addition, the vast majority of employers are required by federal and/or state law to pay overtime to employees who work more than 40 hours per week, unless the employee is exempt. Independent contractors, however, are not entitled to overtime pay. As a result, if an individual is categorized incorrectly, it could mean costly legal and financial consequences for your business.

There is no single determining factor for categorizing an individual as an independent contractor or an employee. The IRS has developed a 20-factor test to help determine the correct employment status; however, there are a handful of factors that are most commonly analyzed to make the determination.

EMPLOYEE	INDEPENDENT CONTRACTOR
Economically dependent on employer	Economically independent
Works for one employer	Provides services to more than one company
Works hours set by employer	Sets own hours
Is given training for work	No training
Works under the control or direction of employer	Works relatively independently
No independent contractor agreement	Independent contractor agreement

Having an independent contractor agreement is good evidence that the worker should be categorized as an independent contractor rather than an employee. As an entrepreneur, it is important to know what makes the difference to minimize your risk of running into unexpected legal or financial hurdles.

Entrepreneur's GUIDE

- 6 -

TRADEMARKS & SERVICE MARKS

TRADEMARKS & SERVICE MARKS

Protecting your brand is key to maintaining a thriving business. Fortunately, the United States federal and state governments provide a means to protect your brand in the form of a trademark (or service mark). A trademark is a word, phrase, symbol, and/or design that identifies and distinguishes the source of the *goods* of one party from those of others. A service mark is a word, phrase, symbol, and/or design that identifies and distinguishes the source of a *service* rather than goods. Trademarks put businesses at a competitive advantage because it assures consistent quality of products and/or services, which leads to greater customer satisfaction and higher sales.

Having a trademark is essential because it is legal protection for the investment in your brand. A state trademark protects your mark within the state that it's registered, while a federal trademark, filed through the United States Patent and Trademark Office (USPTO), is protected throughout the entire United States and its territories and possessions. In addition, a federal trademark registration can be used to stop trademark infringing imports at the U.S. border, but a state trademark

Trademarks & Service Marks

registration cannot. Some specific benefits of having a federally registered trademark include:

- Protects against federal registration of not only identical marks, but also confusingly similar marks
- Provides nationwide notice of ownership of the mark as of the registration date
- Grants the right to use the ® symbol when the mark is used in connection with the goods and services listed in the registration
- Serves as evidence of the valid and exclusive ownership of the mark in connection with the goods and services listed in the registration
- Discourages others from using confusingly similar marks, as your mark will be easy to find within the federal registry
- Prevents others from claiming that their subsequent use of the same mark was in "good faith"

Trademark protection certainly should not be something you think about only after you have a strong brand to protect; it should be in the forefront of your mind when you are initially creating the name and logo for your business. Why so soon? Because some names and logos are much harder to obtain a trademark for than others, and some are not eligible at all. Some names and logos are eligible for trademark protection on the first day of business, while with others, you have to wait several years to even be considered. For these reasons, it's important that you work with a trademark lawyer upfront to assist you with understanding these concepts so you can make the best decisions for your business and brand.

Levels of Trademark Protection

The hierarchy of marks allows for different strengths of protection. At the very bottom are generic marks, which are not protectable by a federal trademark. A generic mark is a word or symbol that is commonly used to describe an entire type of product or service rather than to distinguish one source of a product or service from another. For example, if someone wanted to trademark a brand of hats called "Hats" or a beauty parlor called "The Salon," the trademark application would be denied because the mark is generic. It wouldn't be fair to prevent other hat stores from using the word "hats" in their brand or the word "salon" for a beauty establishment.

The next level is descriptive marks. A descriptive mark describes the product or service that it is attributed to. For instance, a pizza store called "Cheesy Pies" would be a descriptive mark because it merely describes the product that it is selling. In order to receive a trademark for a descriptive mark, it must become distinctive by acquiring "secondary meaning." Secondary meaning is achieved when the mark, through advertising or other exposure, has come to signify that a good or service comes from a particular source. Before a descriptive mark can obtain trademark protection, enough evidence must be gathered and submitted with your trademark application, to the satisfaction of your trademark application examiner, to prove that your mark has acquired secondary meaning. A trademark attorney can help you gather the evidence you need to meet the secondary meaning threshold.

An example of a descriptive mark that has acquired secondary meaning and become protectable as a trademark is the brand name "ChapStick" for lip balm. ChapStick describes the product – a stick for chapped lips. Without secondary meaning, the name "ChapStick" is merely descriptive and not protectable under trademark law. The brand name acquired secondary meaning because after years of sales and advertising, consumers now associate the brand name "ChapStick" with a particular source.

A suggestive mark refers to some characteristic of the goods, but requires a leap of the imagination to get from the mark to the product. It doesn't exactly describe the product or service, but with some thought, consumers can likely figure out the creative connection between the mark and the product or service. For example, the brand name "Penguin" for refrigerators is suggestive. The word "penguin" does not describe a refrigerator, but because both penguins and refrigerators are associated with really cold environments, it is a suggestive mark. Suggestive marks, and the following two types of marks, do not need secondary meaning to be registered.

An arbitrary mark is a common word or phrase, but the meaning of that particular word or phrase is not related to the product or service. "Apple" is an example of an arbitrary mark because it is a real word, but it is not related to goods or services in the technology field, which is what the company sells.

Finally, there's the fanciful mark. A fanciful mark gets the strongest trademark protection because the brand name or logo is a made up word or image by the brand owner and therefore, the sole meaning and association is dependent upon that product or service. Examples include "Exxon" and its relationship to petroleum and "Kodak" for photography. Both "Exxon" and

"Kodak" are made up words, and due to the creativity of the brand owner, these name get the highest trademark protection. Although fanciful marks have the greatest protection, it can be expensive to brand a made up word to the ideal level of wide-spread consumer familiarity.

Trademark Eligibility

A brand that is inherently distinctive (fanciful, arbitrary, or suggestive) is eligible for trademark protection once it is used in commerce in connection with the good or service. For federal trademark protection, the mark must be used in interstate commerce (across state lines). According to the Trademark Act, "the term 'use in commerce' means the bona fide use of a mark in the ordinary course of trade..." Although the law does not explain the exact meaning of that vague definition, legal precedent has taught us that a sham sale or transfer of goods for the purpose of trademark registration will not suffice (i.e. sale of a few dollars' worth of goods to a cooperating third party who immediately returned the goods to the seller).

Now, if you want to reserve your mark but have not used it in commerce yet, you can file an intent-to-use federal trademark application. An intent-to-use application is a federal trademark application that reserves the mark for an initial period of six months. Within that six months, you must submit a statement of use to the USPTO along with applicable filing fees. If you need more time to actually use the mark in commerce, you may request up to four additional six-month extensions. However, the USPTO will only grant your extension requests upon a showing of "good cause" as to why the mark has not yet been used. If you do not file your statement of use within the required time period, then your application will be considered abandoned.

Securing a trademark for the name and logo of your business is essential to building and protecting your brand. It prevents others from capitalizing off of your brand investment and assures consistent quality. This is important because, among other things, if you decide to add another product or service to your business, consumers will be more comfortable trying it due to the trustworthy brand you've built and protected. The great thing about trademarks is that they last forever, so long as you are protecting it. So if you have a registered trademark, be sure to use the ® symbol to let the public know that you own it and to deter others from using a similar brand. Lastly, make sure that you take action if you become aware of any unlawful use of your trademark.

Entrepreneur's GUIDE

- 7 -

COPYRIGHT

COPYRIGHT

Like trademarks, copyright is also a form of protection for your brand. Copyright protection is provided by the laws of the United States Constitution to the authors of "original works of authorship," including literary, dramatic, musical, artistic, and certain other intellectual works. These works of authorship must be "fixed in a tangible medium," which means that they must be attached to something you can touch (i.e. written down, recorded, on a canvas, etc.) and be more than just ideas or suggestions. In addition, the work must contain at least some creativity. The 1976 Copyright Act gives the copyright owner the exclusive right to do, and to authorize others to do, the following:

- Reproduce the work in copies
- Prepare derivative works based upon the work
- Distribute copies of the work to the public by sale or other transfer of ownership, or by rental, lease, or lending
- Perform the work publicly, in the case of literary, musical, dramatic, and choreographic works, pantomimes, and motion pictures and other audio visual works
- Display the work publicly

- Perform the work publicly (in the case of sound recordings) by means of a digital audio transmission

While it is true that copyright is mostly used to protect works of artists and authors, it is actually quite relevant for almost every business owner, regardless of the type of business. Most businesses have a logo that they use to build their brand in connection with the goods or services that they offer. In addition, most business owners do not create their logo themselves; they usually have someone else who is skilled in graphic design create it for them. According to copyright law, the person that creates the art (in this case the logo), owns it – regardless if the business owner paid for it.

Copyright protection exists from the moment that the work is created and the copyright in the work immediately becomes the property of the author who created it. There are, however, two ways that business owners can obtain ownership of the copyright for their logo.

1. **Work Made for Hire – by employment.** The business owner owns the copyright in the logo if the logo was created by an employee within the scope of his or her employment. For example, if the graphic designer in your

company's marketing department created the logo, which is likely within the employee's scope of employment, depending on the job description. However, if you own a construction company, and one of your workers happens to be a great artist and draws a logo for the business that you start to use, the worker owns the copyright, because creating logos for the business is not within his or her scope of employment.

2. **Copyright Assignment.** If the logo design does not fall under a work for hire by employment, you can have an agreement drafted assigning the rights and ownership in the logo from the designer to you. This assignment agreement will allow you to register the copyright in your name (or better yet, in your business's name), and will give you all rights as the owner of the full copyright.

Along with protecting the rights in your logo, copyright also protects other intellectual property for your business, such as manuals, your website layout and wording, marketing materials, written and audio visual advertisements, handbooks, and more.

Copyright Registration

Although the author of the work automatically has a copyright in it as soon as it is created, it is highly recommended to register the copyright with the United States Copyright Office. Registering your copyright provides additional benefits such as:

- Establishes a public record of the copyright holder's ownership
- Provides sufficient evidence in court concerning the validity of the copyright if registered before or within five years of publication
- Enables the copyright owner to sue for infringement in federal court
- Entitles the copyright owner to seek statutory damages and attorney's fees in federal court. Statutory damages range from $750 to $150,000 per work that is infringed. Without registration, only actual damages and profit will be awarded, which can be very difficult to prove.
- Protects against the importation of infringing copies when the registration is recorded with U.S. Customs

Copyright is a great tool to ensure that the intellectual property that you create for your business is protected. It deters others from stealing your materials and provides legal recourse in the unfortunate event that it occurs.

Entrepreneur's GUIDE

- 8 -

PATENTS

PATENTS

Securing a patent may also be valuable you if your business involves a new invention. A patent is a grant of property right, issued by the United States Patent and Trademark Office, which gives the right to exclude others from making, using, selling, or importing the invention. According to patent law, any person who "invents or discovers any new and useful process, machine, manufacture, or composition of matter, or any new and useful improvement thereof, may obtain a patent," subject to the conditions and requirements of the law.

U.S. patents are protectable in the United States, U.S. territories, and U.S. possessions. In order to be eligible for a patent, your product, process, design, or discovery must be (1) new, (2) useful, and (3) nonobvious.

Types of Patents

The three relevant types of patents for entrepreneurs are utility patents, design patents, and provisional patents.

Utility Patent

A utility patent, which lasts for 20 years from the date that the patent application was filed, protects the useful or functional aspects of a product, process, or method. A few examples of products and processes that may be protectable by utility patents include medical devices, tools, machines, furniture parts, automobile or machine parts, software, electrical circuits, computers, toys, pharmaceuticals, chemical compounds, methods of treatment, manufacturing processes, and certain types of methods of doing business.

Design Patent

A design patent, which is valid for 15 years after it is granted, protects the way a product (or other matter) looks, such as its shape and configuration. For example, The Coca-Cola Company has a design patent on its unique design for the Coca-Cola bottle shape:

Provisional Patent

Lastly, a provisional patent application will never be examined, but is used to establish a priority date. It is designed to give the inventor more time to decide if he wants to pursue a utility or design patent application, which requires more work and is more expensive. A provisional patent application involves a simple description of a well-developed idea along with any applicable drawings.

Although it is somewhat simple to get a provisional patent, its upgrade is time-sensitive. If a design or utility patent is not filed within one year of the provisional patent application, then it will automatically become abandoned. The only exception is that if a utility or design patent application is filed within two months of the provisional patent expiration date, then the inventor may retain its priority date by filing a petition, which must include a statement that the delay was unintentional and the required petition fee.

Filing for a utility or design patent can be a very lengthy, tedious and detail-oriented process. Before filing the application, it is important to do a thorough patent search to make sure that your invention is new.

Keep in mind that an inventor has only one year after his first public use or offer for sale of the invention within which to file a patent application. In addition, if the inventor describes the invention in a printed publication (i.e. advertisement, websites, brochures) he/she also has one year from that publication in which to file the patent application. If an application is not filed within that period, a valid patent for the invention cannot be obtained.

Successfully obtaining a patent is a great accomplishment and there are many ways to financially benefit. You can sell your patent to a third party for monetary compensation, license your patent to one or more parties for a percentage of sales, or exclusively manufacturer and sell your invention on your own. A patent is a valuable asset and is needed to protect you from others benefiting from the hard work that you've put in to make your invention come to life.

Entrepreneur's GUIDE

- 9 -

LICENSING

LICENSING

Licensing is a very relevant topic for entrepreneurs. A license is a special permission to do something on or with somebody else's property. A license granted by the owner (the "licensor") of a patent or a copyright gives the license holder (the "licensee") a limited right to reproduce, sell, display, or distribute the work. Likewise, the owner of a trademark may give a third party a license to use the owner's mark (i.e. brand name or logo) in connection with other goods or services. These intellectual property licenses usually require that the licensee pay a fee to the licensor in exchange for use of the property.

When doing a licensing deal, it's important to consider whether you want to grant (or receive) an exclusive license or a non-exclusive license. An exclusive license means that no person or company other than the named licensee can exploit the rights granted. Conversely, a non-exclusive license grants to the licensee the right to use the intellectual property, but means that the licensor remains free to allow any number of other licensees to also exploit the same material. Exclusive licenses are often more valuable that non-exclusive licenses and can provide a steep competitive edge for the licensee's business.

| Licensing

Here's a real life example of licensing in business. The NFL 2K series and EA Sports' Madden had been competitors for some time in the gaming industry. Both brands had a non-exclusive license to use the trademarks and other intellectual property of the National Football League in their respective games. In or around 2004, the NFL 2K series started selling a superior product for a reduced price. EA Sports panicked, leading them to cut the price of the Madden game in order to keep up with (or surpass) NFL 2K's sales. In response to the retail price war, EA Sports decided to pay the National Football League for an exclusive license to prevent the NFL 2K series and any other company from using the NFL's intellectual property (team names, logos, etc.) in the gaming industry, and thereby allowing EA Sports to price their game without the pressure of competition.

As you can see, licensing deals can make a big difference in the profits and popularity of your business.

Key Terms in Licensing Deals

When negotiating a licensing deal, it is important to pay close attention to the following terms:

- **Term:** Tells the length of time that the license will be granted.

- **Endorsements:** Determines whether or not the owner of the property (i.e. the copyrighted material, the logo, etc.) will be required to endorse the product or service of the licensee.

- **Exclusivity:** The parties must decide whether it will be an exclusive or non-exclusive license. Exclusive licenses generally cost more than non-exclusive licenses.

- **Territory:** This tells the geographic location (i.e. the state, the county, the world) where the licensee can use the property. The greater the geographic area, the more leverage the licensor has for higher compensation.

- **Quality Standards:** Provides a certain standard that the licensee must adhere to for products or services that contain the licensor's property. This is important to help ensure that the property is not devalued by being associated with the licensee.

- **Approval Rights:** Determines whether the licensor will have the right to approve the products or services that the licensee uses in connection with the licensed property.

- **Compensation:** Tells how the licensor will be paid for use of its property. Common forms of compensation include a flat fee, royalties (which are a percentage of sales), or a combination of both.

- **Confidentiality:** It's almost inevitable that the licensee will learn some confidential information about the licensor and/or its property, and maybe vice-versa. The confidentiality clause will make the parties promise not to disclose any confidential information that may be revealed to the other as a result of the licensing deal.

Licensing deals can propel your business by allowing your property to have exposure to a larger audience and expanding your sources of revenue. By obtaining a license, you will legally be able to profit off of the brand that a successful individual or company has built. This is also an incentive for you as a business owner to build a strong brand, because it will attract others to seek a licensing deal with you.

Entrepreneur's GUIDE

- 10 -

PROTECTING YOUR LIMITED LIABILITY

PROTECTING YOUR LIMITED LIABILITY

As I mentioned in the chapter on business entity structures, forming your business entity (LLC, Corporation, etc.) will grant you limited liability, which means that you as the business owner will (generally) not be liable for the debts and financial liabilities of the company. So, for example, if the business takes out a loan and defaults on the loan, then the lender cannot seek recourse by attaching your personal assets such as your house and car, unless you personally guaranteed the loan. Likewise, if someone sues your business for a financial liability, the law does not allow them to also include you as a defendant to the lawsuit just because you are the owner.

While having limited liability can provide great peace of mind as you are managing your business and entering into new business transactions, you must make sure that you are operating in a way that protects your limited liability. If not, then creditors or plaintiffs in lawsuits can "pierce the corporate veil," which means disregard the business entity and pursue their claims against you as an individual.

There are several things you can do to protect your limited liability. Here are three best practices:

Bank Account

Make sure you have a business bank account that is separate from your personal bank account. All funds that you receive for your business should be deposited in the business bank account. All business expenses should be paid from your business bank account or business credit card. In addition, pay yourself from the funds in your business bank account on a scheduled and consistent basis. Overall, keep business and personal finances separate.

Contracts

All contracts that you enter into on behalf of or for the benefit of your business should be in the name of the business. This means that the business is a party to the contract and not you as an individual.

Corporate Formalities

You must adhere to certain corporate formalities in order to protect your limited liability. For example, corporations must have bylaws, a board of directors, regular board meetings, and meetings minutes. If your corporation is operating without these, then it's limited liability may be at stake. For this reason, I recommend LLCs for new entrepreneurs because there are less corporate formalities to adhere to – you already have enough to

| Protecting Your Limited Liability 61

handle. Keep in mind that filing your annual registrations and maintaining an operating agreement for your LLC provide great evidence that your limited liability should be respected.

Overall, remember to keep the business of your company separate from you as an individual. Do not commingle business and personal funds, maintain proper business contracts, and adhere to corporate formalities, if required.

ated to increase, (c) continuous modification of the technology is constrained by the high cost of high technology R&D and the need to work at the fringes of what is theoretically achievable, and (d) the rapid rise in the cost of technology has spread throughout the economies of the developed world, causing price hyperinflation in those areas where high technology has played a dominant role, notably in medical services, the military, and the space and energy industries.

Technology Management is a new discipline. Major universities, including Sloan, Wharton, Harvard, Stanford, and MIT, are beginning to offer courses. Increased attention is being paid to what goes on inside a company when a new technology is introduced: how it is accommodated; how the company ensures that the new technology is fully exploited; and how the new technology is prevented from creating a turbulence so great that employees cannot adapt.

Important aspects of Technology Management include: the assessment of emerging new technologies, their market potential, their limitations, their life cycle, their associated costs, and the development of a comprehensive corporate strategy by means of which the company can fully exploit the emerging technology while disposing of the mature technologies being replaced.

A consideration of Technology Management must also include an analysis of the obsolescence curve for the particular high technology. How long will it take for the technology to be outdated by some newer technology? How extensively and intensively will it be used during its life cycle? What are the options for modifying and upgrading the basic technology? Can it be modularized so that as parts of it are outdated they can be replaced by newer modules without replacing the entire technology?

FINAL THOUGHT

In this chapter we have reviewed the basic functional building blocks of technology commercialization: R&D/Engineering, Production, Marketing, Finance, and Administration. We have looked at the functions themselves, at how they inter-

FINAL THOUGHT

For me, becoming an entrepreneur was one of the best decisions that I have made in my life. It has allowed me to build a life that I used to dream of, and continue to build for even greater possibilities. Before I opened my law firm, I remember having a burning desire to work for myself. I did not like the idea of an employer benefitting from my unique talents and skills more than I was. I had no doubt that I was capable of achieving something much greater; but of course, at times, fear held me back from being as aggressive with pursuing my dreams as I should have been. Over that time period and looking back now, I know that what got me to overcome that fear was knowledge and preparation.

I encourage you to be proactive in obtaining the knowledge you need to be successful in your business venture(s). Feed your mind with new information each day and make a solid plan to implement your business idea. Now that you have the basics of what your business needs legally, integrate what you have learned from this book into your plan. Entrepreneurship can be life-changing for you and your family, and it all grows from a solid business and legal foundation.

DAYNATHOMASLAW.COM